MIRACLES for RICHARD

Doris Straut

ISBN 979-8-88832-408-0 (paperback)
ISBN 979-8-88832-409-7 (digital)

Copyright © 2023 by Doris Straut

All rights reserved. No part of this publication may be reproduced, distributed, or transmitted in any form or by any means, including photocopying, recording, or other electronic or mechanical methods without the prior written permission of the publisher. For permission requests, solicit the publisher via the address below.

Christian Faith Publishing
832 Park Avenue
Meadville, PA 16335
www.christianfaithpublishing.com

Printed in the United States of America

To my husband, Nelson, and four children
Denise, Christopher, John, and Richard

When I knew I was expecting my fourth child, I asked the Lord if we could have another girl (we already had two boys and a girl). Antibodies were building up, and I had to have my blood checked every week. I had RH-negative blood, and my husband had RH-positive, which sometimes caused "blue babies" needing blood transfusions at birth. So I knew God was telling me I was having a boy.

All our children had blond hair and blue eyes. My husband had black hair and brown eyes, so I asked the Lord if He would grant my prayer for our son to have auburn hair and brown eyes. Mark 11:24 says, "Therefore I tell you, whatsoever you ask for believe that you have received it, and it will be yours." This was the first of many miracles for Richard.

"One a punce a time" was the way Richard would begin telling his version of the fairy tale *Little Red Riding Hood* or, as Richard said, "Little Redwood Riding Hood." At two years of age, sitting on my lap, he would entertain anyone who would listen with his version of fairy tales. He always had an enchanted audience. He never met a stranger.

He would talk to people in other cars, when we would be stopped at a red light or side by side in traffic. They would always respond and smile at him. Once he saw a police officer in his patrol car, and he yelled, "Hi, Mr. Policeman!"

The police officer yelled back, "Hi, little man!"

He loved it.

Around the same time, two years of age, he told me he looked like God and that he had lived with God before he came to live with me. I explained to him that the Bible said we were all made in the image of God, and that, yes, he looked like God. Then he said, "But I do look like God. He has hair and eyes like me."

Who knows?

We had a creek behind our house with a small water-fall over rocks. In the summer, the boys would play all day in the creek area (I was always worried about snakes because we had seen some there, but I am sure the snakes fled with all the noise the boys made).

They would play all day, coming in for lunch, and then back to the creek again. The minute they came in for the day, I would take them straight to the bathroom for their baths. I would say, "Boys, stop taking off your clothes down to your skivvies and sliding down the waterfall!" They were amazed that I knew that they had done just that. They didn't know that I saw two little holes on the back of their underwear. Where they had slid down the falls so many times, it had worn two holes in the seat of their underwear!

I had taught them to never play with fire! Or so I thought I had taught them to never play with fire. They would come in for the day, after being outside for most of the day, and I would say, "Boys, I have told you many times not to play with fire! Let me have the matches you have, and don't ever play with fire again or else!

They would say to each other, "How did she know we were building a fire? She knows everything!"

They didn't know they smelled like smoke!

While Richard was in the first grade of school, he was always surprising us with something new. He had art

MIRACLES FOR RICHARD

projects displayed at our local shopping mall, winning first place in his grade level.

He was called Richie since he was born, and we thought it suited him. One afternoon, he came home from first grade and said, "Mom, I have a big favor to ask of you."

I said, "I will do my best to help you if I can. What is it?"

"Well, I am older now, and I want to be called Richard."

I stifled a laugh and answered solemnly, "I think I can do that."

He said, "I want everyone to call me Richard."

Of course, from that day forward, he was Richard. We had named him Richard because of its meaning—strong in rule, leader, king, strong, brave, hardy!

We experienced revival at our church, and he was attuned to witnessing about Jesus. So he came home from first-grade class at school to tell us that he had told a classmate about Jesus. He was always sharing about Jesus with others. He accepted Jesus Christ as his Lord and Savior and was baptized at the age of eight. John 3:16 says, "For God so loved the world that He gave his only begotten son, that whosoever believeth in him should not perish but have everlasting life."

Richard was unique in that he always obeyed whatever we asked him to do. I would say, "Richard, please pick up your toys. It is time for dinner." And he would immediately do so, which was a shock to us as our older children always had to be told more than once. He was such a pleasure.

My husband's hobby was working on cars. Richard followed him around, asking questions and wanting to help him, learning auto mechanics at an early age (seven). He put a rag in his back pocket, just like his dad did, to wipe his hands when they got oil on them.

Nelson, my husband and Richard's father, had a "creeper" he used when he did oil changes, etc., under the car. Richard wanted to "ride" with him on his creeper. So his dad made him a smaller version of the creeper so that Richard could continue being with his father and learning more about the working of a car.

When Richard was in third grade, his teacher gave them an assignment to write a story. Richard wrote a story about a little mouse that became a hero for saving a whole town from a huge snake. The teacher made his story into a book. He made an "A."

At around nine years of age, he started collecting trains and anything to do with trains, such as bridges, village buildings, houses, churches, people, etc. He used an eight-foot piece of plywood and built train tracks with villages, people, grass, the whole works. It was really a work of art when he finished. He even used our movie camera and made a scary movie using his trains and villages about people disappearing. Very good.

He cut grass for neighbors to make money for these hobbies and did very well for himself to support his hobbies. He even bought a small motorboat to use at our lake place on Lake Lanier. He loved to fish, and this was another of his hobbies.

When he was twelve, he and his best friend, Keven, began shooting off rockets at the playground of their school. They would buy rockets and everything required to help them launch the rockets. Every Saturday morning, we would go with Richard, Keven, and his parents to the school to shoot off the rockets. They would sometimes go so high you couldn't see them until the parachute would bring them back down. There would always be an audience enjoying watching the rockets.

When he was sixteen, he went to work at Burger King, flipping hamburgers to keep his spending money to support his hobbies, then he went to work at a gas station, just down the street, learning more about the mechanics of a car. He did all this while making very good grades at school.

While sixteen, he got his driver's license, and we gave him a red Ford truck. He took good care of his prized possession. He washed, waxed, and kept it in pristine condition. He bought and installed an overhead stereo.

Just after getting his truck, he went to work at Richway, a department store with a garden center, working after school and on weekends. He was working on a Saturday in the garden center, when he looked up through the fence and saw his truck leaving the parking lot. He knew if it was us, we would have told him before taking his truck. A friend happened to be leaving work, and he ran out to catch up with him and asked him if he would take him to follow his car that was being stolen. He said okay.

After getting in his friend's car, he found a knife in the glove compartment, and at the next red light, they caught up with his truck. He jumped out, ran up to the front of his truck, confronted the driver, and shouted for him to get out. The man said, "Hey, dude, I'm just borrowing it."

The light changed, Richard jumped into the back of the truck, and the guy took off. Richard kept yelling for the guy to get out of his truck. He had a big toolbox in the back of his truck, and he said to himself that he would take out a hammer and break the glass, climb into his truck, hit the guy on the head, and get his truck back. By then, they had stopped at another red light.

This red light happened to be at the exit to the interstate, heading to Alabama. With no more red lights, he would not be stopping again.

A police officer, who was just getting off work, was in a vehicle facing them at the light. He saw Richard standing in the back of the truck, yelling for the man to get out of his truck. The police officer got out of his vehicle with his nightstick and stood in front of Richard's truck and told the guy to get out of the truck so he could determine who owned the truck. Richard rattled off the VIN and the tag number to prove the truck was his. When the officer looked in the truck, he saw a screwdriver stuck in the ignition. He arrested the car thief.

It so happened that the guy arrested was in a car theft ring from Alabama that they had been trying to identify. The theft ring members were stealing red cars and trucks and taking them to Alabama to sell (they didn't need car titles at that time in Alabama), and the red cars and trucks were in great demand.

The judge in Gwinnett County and police officers all said Richard was a hero for helping bust the car theft ring. He was a hero there and at the high school the next school day, where word had gotten out that he had helped bust a car theft ring.

Challenges seemed to follow Richard. One night, he was at a friend's house until around ten-thirty. Leaving to come home, he backed out of their driveway and was hit by a car with no lights on. He was shocked as he was always so careful. His friend's dad joined him, and they chased the car to just a few yards down the road, where the car that hit him was in a ditch.

They confronted the driver who had a broken arm and was so drunk he didn't realize his arm was dangling.

They called the local police to register the incident and got his insurance information. He was an FBI agent and later threatened us because he was FBI. We told him it did not matter because he was a hit-and-run violator. Needless to say, he lost his job.

Richard's strong faith in his Lord and Savior, Jesus Christ, continued to strengthen as he faced even more challenges. John 14:1 says, "Let not your Heart be troubled, ye believe in God believe also in me."

Richard enlisted in the Georgia National Guard in 1985, after attending two years of college. Going into the military police training at Fort McClellan, Alabama, where he did his basic training. He also joined the Atlanta Police Department after boot camp and went through the police academy to become a full-fledged police officer. While working, he attended OCS in Macon, Georgia, commuting on weekends. He was learning to fly helicopters. He graduated a second lieutenant from OCS. His plan was to go to Fort Rucker, Alabama. His goal was to become an astronaut.

After his third year with the police department, the tragedy struck.

He was due to attend summer camp with the National Guard in May 1989. He also had a brother who was getting married on Saturday, May sixth. He already had permission to come home from summer camp for the wedding as he was to be his brother's best man.

The day before the wedding, the summer camp was cancelled (which had never happened before) because of a problem with a pin in the rotor blade of the helicopter. Therefore, Richard was released to come home.

On Sunday, the day after the wedding, he called in to his office to see if he was needed. They said they did need him to work Sunday night on the evening shift.

While on duty that night, he answered a call that a man was refusing to pay a cab fare. When he arrived, he talked with the cab driver, then went to the house of the man refusing to pay the cab fare. When the man answered the door, Richard asked him to step out to his patrol car to talk with him about the situation with the cab fare. When Richard turned to head back to his car, the man hit him in the back of his head, stunning him, and he was dragged into the man's house. The man grabbed his police gun and began shooting at him, hitting him in the head. Richard had packed his bullets himself, making hollow-point bullets, which should have blown off the side of his head when the bullets hit his head. The bullet had lodged in his brain, and he was bleeding profusely. The man continued shooting at him, missing, and hitting the floor tiles, breaking them into little pieces that were hitting Richard in the face, cutting his face.

During the scuffle, Richard tried to reach for his second gun that was located on his ankle but couldn't seem to reach for it and, at that point, couldn't understand why (he did not know then that he was paralyzed on his left side by the bullet in the brain).

Richard tried to radio for help, and someone overrode his call for help with a request to go to dinner. The dispatcher knew someone was calling for help and did a roll call. When Richard didn't respond, they sent help right away.

The man who shot him was a Black Muslim and had vowed to kill a police officer the day before.

MIRACLES FOR RICHARD

The call for help arrived in just a few minutes with an ambulance in tow. They placed Richard on a gurney and rushed him to Grady Memorial Hospital, to the trauma unit, noted to be the best in the country.

They arrived at Grady in seven minutes, and Richard heard someone say, "Boy, that man is dead and just doesn't realize it." He didn't know they were talking about him.

They rushed him into surgery, where they needed to tie off the arteries, where they were severed by the bullet and bleeding into the brain. When blood touches the brain cells, it kills the cells, so the neurosurgeons were trying to locate the ones that were severed to tie them off. They found two, tied them off, and were looking for one more. They couldn't seem to find the third artery and were getting ready to close him up, when they found the third and final artery.

Shot point blank, officer makes heroic return

DORIS STRAUT

Wounded Policeman Is Praised By Officials

From Page B1

FLOYD JILLSON/Staff

Harold A. Davis was charged with aggravated assault in the Sunday shooting of Atlanta police Officer Richard Kelley Straut.

hospital spokesman Jim Driscoll.

Several members of Officer Straut's Army National Guard unit offered donations of rare B-negative blood, the wounded officer's type, to replenish Red Cross supplies. A second lieutenant in B Company of the 1st/244th Aviation Regiment based in Winder, Officer Straut was awaiting orders to attend helicopter flight school.

"He was a good young officer," said Capt. James Wilkie, his company commander. "We're saying our prayers and hoping it works out."

Atlanta police investigators are still trying to determine exactly what happened Sunday evening when Officer Straut entered the foyer of Mr. Davis's apartment at 886 Booker T. Washington Drive N.W., where he and his wife have lived for 10 years.

"We assume the officer tried to find out why Mr. Davis wouldn't pay his taxi fare, and a struggle ensued in which Mr. Davis managed to take possession of two weapons the officer had, his service revolver and a backup weapon," said homicide Lt. Horace Walker.

At least two, perhaps three shots were fired, Lt. Walker said, but only one struck Officer Straut. The alleged assailant jumped out a side window and fled up a hill to a neighboring complex, taking refuge in a crawl space under an apartment building at 106 Hilltop Circle.

The fugitive demanded that he speak to police detective and fellow Muslim Wali Kareem, said Maj. W.W. Holley, whose SWAT units were dispatched to the scene and ordered residents of the building and surrounding units to evacuate.

"We made things clear to him that he had to come and face what he has done, there was no other way," said Major Holley. But authorities called on Detective Kareem.

Mr. Kareem, now a detective assigned to the Atlanta city schools, said he had known Mr. Davis for at least seven years, since he was sent to Mr. Davis's home to quell a dispute with a neighbor. "We built up a relationship over the years," said Mr. Kareem. "He's a Muslim and I'm a Muslim and he didn't want to surrender to anyone but me.

"He wanted to make sure they weren't playing games, and he wanted to see my face," demanding the officer stick his head into the crawl space. "I didn't want to do that because I wasn't sure how he would react. I showed him my ring, it's one that Muslims wear, and he began to ask me questions that only I would know the answers to.

"That didn't take long; in a couple of minutes he said, 'OK, I'll come out.'"

THE WALL STREET JOURNAL.

Kelly Greene
Staff Reporter

Jan. 16, 2006

Dear Richard,

Thanks so much for your help with the story — please keep me posted on what happens next!

Regards,
Kelly Greene

DOWJONES

We were told that Richard probably would not make it, and if he did, he would be a "vegetable." I told the young doctor that wasn't true because we were praying to our God for a miracle. We had already experienced several of God's miracles.

We had been using the waiting room that was continually filled with our family and friends. Other patients' families had nowhere to wait, so we were given a doctor's quarters on the fifteenth floor. We had assigned police officers around the clock to be with us.

My good friend, Jane Schwartz, brought us food every day while Richard was at Grady Hospital. And Scott Bennett, a friend and an Atlanta Police Officer, brought us breakfast from McDonald's, given to him free of charge.

I was able to go down to the trauma unit to see Richard every two hours for about ten minutes. I would return from seeing Richard, devastated and crying uncontrollably and would go into my bedroom. I knew we were being prayed for by many, many people. And as I was crying, I would suddenly be overwhelmed with a feeling of something coming over me, lifting me up. I literally felt as though someone was lifting me up, and I felt so lighthearted.

I would then leave my room and go into the sitting room, where a police officer would be sitting. I am sure they were surprised by my happy spirit. So whenever you hear the phrase being lifted up, it can be literal. God is good.

When I would go visit with Richard, I had to rely on the Lord for strength. He had a tube screwed into his head, a neck brace, and IVs in each arm. He looked gray. And I could tell he was paralyzed on his left side. He also had a tube in his nose.

He would take my hand, even though he was sedated, and write "hose in nose" in my hand. I knew what he was trying to convey. So I whispered in his ear that I knew he was a very strong young man and that he could endure this for a little while as they were trying to do everything for him to recover. It broke my heart.

I would say a prayer in his ear and quote scripture every time I visited him, encouraging him the best I knew how.

I was in the halls and elevators so much everyone learned that I was Richard's mom, and they would ask about him and tell me they were praying for him.

After two weeks had passed, I went down, one morning, and they had moved him to another area of the hospital. Richard had always told me that the trauma unit of Grady Hospital was best in the USA, but if they ever put him in the other part of the hospital, *get him out of there!*

I was directed to his room and found him in a puddle of sweat, and he had a fever. I was very upset.

I called for a nurse to have his sheets changed. They said they didn't have time right then. I told them to give me the sheets, and I would change them, that he didn't need to be so wet with a fever. They got upset with me but changed the sheets. I immediately called our doctors and arranged for him to be sent to Emory University Hospital the next morning.

We went by ambulance the next morning to Emory Hospital, where he immediately received the care he needed. Soon after, they began rehab to get him sitting up. It was very hard for him as he had been lying in bed for three weeks.

He was on TV and in all the papers daily as they followed his recovery progress.

MIRACLES FOR RICHARD

I had been massaging his left side every day since he entered the trauma unit the day he was shot, hoping it might help him.

While we were with Richard at Grady Hospital, friends from church, organized by Jeanette Singleton, a good friend, sent food to our family daily; and friends, teachers, and parents from Smoke Rise School, where I worked, sent food and helped in many, many ways.

We moved him to Emory Rehab Center, where they evaluated him, not giving much hope on his walking again.

They began a six-week rehab. He told me that because of the massaging I gave him, he was beginning to move his left foot and toes, that the massaging had felt so good.

The rehab doctor, in front of Richard, said that he would never fly again and probably not walk.

I told him that he must not know our God because we were praying that he would walk again, and we believed that God would perform another of His miracles and that Richard would walk again.

Richard, in turn, told him that he would not just walk out of his hospital, but he would run out.

We brought him home to our house since he wasn't able as yet to be on his own at his home.

We enrolled him at Atlanta Rehab to continue his rehabilitation.

While there, one of his friends came by to take him to lunch. They were gone about one and a half hours, making him late for his next class.

The leader of the class reprimanded him for being late. Richard was humiliated and very upset as he had not seen his friends on a social level in many weeks. Richard shared that with me that evening, when he came home.

13

Needless to say, he didn't want me to do anything about that situation, but you don't mess with a mama bear. I called the rehab and told them that Richard was not to have that class and that particular leader was not to be over Richard any longer. Richard continued to improve mentally and physically.

The doctors had given Richard a "boot" to support his left foot and ankle. He hated it. It was very uncomfortable for him, so he began to walk without it. He aced the rehab and wanted to go back to work.

You could place your fist in the indention in Richard's head where the bullet entered and bone was removed for surgery. You could even see his heartbeat. His brain was unprotected, so I called a friend, Joann Bakay, whose husband was a neurosurgeon, Dr. Roy Bakay. I made an appointment for Richard to have a plate placed in his head to cover the indention. It was a successful surgery. His beautiful wavy hair covers the huge scar.

The Atlanta Police Department did not realize how persistent Richard could be. He fought every way possible, even qualifying with his gun, which he did (surprising everyone).

Richard was awarded the Georgia Medal of Valor at a ceremony at the Georgia National Guard Post at Winder, Georgia, by General Blandford.

Continuing to do his duties at the Atlanta Police Department, Richard took the sergeants' test and became Sgt. Richard Straut, proving himself able to continue his career as a police officer with only a little paralysis on his left side with no memory loss. Praise the Lord.

Later on, he passed the lieutenants test but did not get appointed because of lack of openings.

He also decided to finish his college education and chose to attend Brenau University in Gainesville, Georgia. He continued working and attending Brenau three evenings a week, driving from Atlanta to Gainesville to attend. He graduated cum laude with a degree in criminal justice.

Friends of ours, Jack and Meg Mumpower, came to our home every Wednesday evening, for several weeks, to help Richard with his balance. Jack has a black belt in Aikido martial arts. He taught Richard self-defense, helping him in many ways, including his balance.

In the early 1990s, Richard became a member of the Police Benevolent Association (PBA). After several years of being a member, he was elected president of the PBA. Under his leadership, he accomplished many advantages for his fellow police officers, helped gain equity for Black officers who were denied access to the pension, and he cowrote the pension plan, which increased the police officers' pension plan by 1 percent, which is 80 percent of their salary.

Richard spoke to classes of elementary school children, where he shared his experiences. He encouraged them to become leaders by first learning to follow orders before being able to give orders. And the first step was to take orders from their parents. We had many responses from parents that he had made a real difference in their children's lives.

He spoke at churches, and, at one point, he was invited to speak to a convention of doctors in Macon, Georgia. They were amazed by his recovery.

We learned the summer Olympics were to be in Atlanta in 1996. I decided to write a letter to the Olympics committee to nominate Richard in hopes he might be selected to carry the torch.

MIRACLES FOR RICHARD

OFFICE OF LIEUTENANT GOVERNOR
240 STATE CAPITOL
ATLANTA, GEORGIA 30334
(404) 656-5030

PIERRE HOWARD
LIEUTENANT GOVERNOR

July 31, 1996

Mr. Richard Straut
515 N. Hairston Rd.
Stone Mountain, Georgia 30083

Dear Richard:

    Congratulations on your selection and successful run as an Olympic Relay torch-bearer. We are proud to have citizens of your distinction representing our state in history.

    Your unique and daily contributions to improving the quality of life in Georgia have greatly enhanced the success and legacy of the Centennial Olympic Games. Please know that your efforts are admired and appreciated throughout our state.

    If I can ever be of service to you in the future, I hope you will call on me at our State Capitol office. The telephone number is (404) 656-5030.

Warmest regards,

Pierre Howard

PH:gl

DORIS STRAUT

DORIS STRAUT

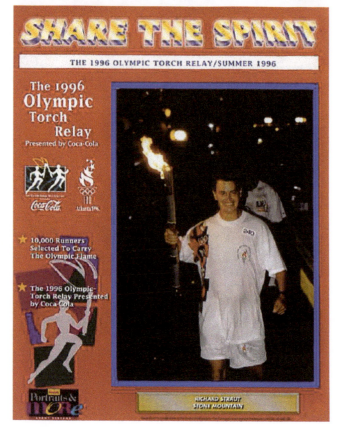

MIRACLES FOR RICHARD

DORIS STRAUT

COMMITTEES:
Children and Youth, Vice Chairman
Education
Governmental Operations
Judiciary

SUBCOMMITTEES:
Libraries, Chairman
Merit System

The State Senate
Atlanta, Georgia 30334

July 31, 1989

Mr. Richard Straut
515 N. Hairston
Stone Mountain, GA

Dear Richard:

I am so glad to hear of your continued recovery from the bullet wound you received in the line of duty. Your courage and determination reflect what a fine and dedicated police officer you are to the City of Atlanta and all Georgia citizens.

My best goes to you and your family as you face this difficult time. With your positive attitude and zest for life, the future looks promising and hopeful.

Thank you for being the kind of person we and our children can all strive to be.

Sincerely,

Joe Burton

JAB/cj

MIRACLES FOR RICHARD

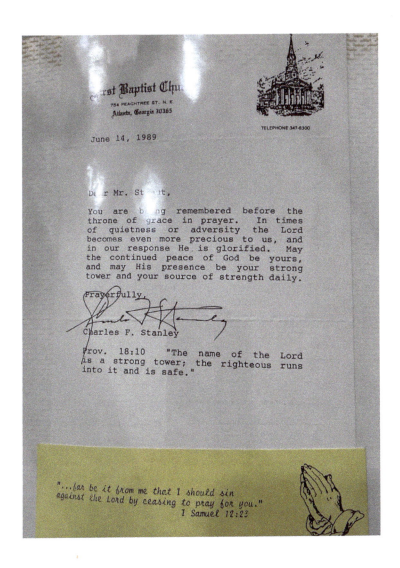

A couple of weeks later, we received a notice that, indeed, Richard had been selected to carry the torch. Not only to carry it but also to light the cauldron in the city of Stone Mountain, Georgia.

We were elated! What an honor. We were given all the instructions, and I was given an Olympic flag to cheer Richard on as he carried the torch.

The final instructions were that he would be running the last one-half mile into the city of Stone Mountain to light the cauldron at 3:00 a.m. *Wow*, I hadn't seen 3:00 a.m. since I was a teenager!

They picked Richard up on a bus with all the other torch carriers to drop them off where they were to begin their "leg" of the race. Everyone on the bus asked Richard, "Why are you the one lighting the cauldron?"

When he told them his experience of being shot in the head, they said, "Yes. You really do deserve to light the cauldron!"

By 2:00 a.m., everyone was lined up on both sides of the street that led into Stone Mountain, getting all excited.

I was very surprised to see so many of my friends, church friends, our children's friends, relatives, parents, and children from Smoke Rise Elementary School, where I worked, all there to support Richard. Of course, our children and grandchildren were there! What a wonderful experience.

Richard also carried the Paralympic torch to the Atlanta Braves Stadium of the Summer 1996 Olympics, which was a great honor for Richard. He has both torches he carried on his walls at his home.

Richard purchased both torches and had them mounted on plaques and displays them in his home.

Richard has been retired for three years and is enjoying retirement in his home on Lake Lanier.

About the Author

Doris Straut grew up in Avondale Estates, Georgia, in a wonderful Christian home. She was a secretary to two Baptist churches for several years before becoming an office manager for an elementary school. Doris taught a lady's Sunday school class for thirty years and led a children's choir for many years. She enjoyed singing in the church choir, a double trio and a mixed quartet. Doris has been married to her husband, Nelson, for sixty-six years, raising four children: Denise, Chris, Johnny, and Richard. They have seven grandchildren and eight great-grandchildren. Doris is retired, living in Daytona Beach, Florida, and enjoys playing bridge. She has been writing this book for several years in her mind, and she has finally put it to paper. Doris hopes it touches your life in some small way.

Printed in the USA
CPSIA information can be obtained
at www.ICGtesting.com
LVHW052329201223
766988LV00111B/6366